A Realm of Her Own

Shreya Siju

Presentation by *BookLeaf Publishing*

Web: www.bookleafpub.com

E-mail: info@bookleafpub.com

ISBN: 9789363319462

First edition 2024

*To all those who have the willpower to
create, you are the driving force for
generations to come.*

ACKNOWLEDGEMENT

This book is known as the living proof of the support I've received along the way from many others. Their constant appreciation is my motivation, my reason to write, and have a smile on my face every day.

My father, someone I'd like to believe is a different version of me that contains my similar personality and nature, has been a guiding light in my journey.

My mother, an illustrious figure who has helped me exemplify my confidence in portraying my flaws to anyone and everyone.

My sister, a best friend is described as the sunshine on a cloudy day, or the relaxing heat from a cozy campfire after experiencing the winter cold.

To all those who support me in my writing abilities, you are the backbone for my reason to continue writing.

PREFACE

A warm welcome to, "A Realm of Her Own", a compilation of poems that traverse through an individual's labyrinth of emotions as well as the serenity of nature, all woven by the creative spirit.

Within the flip of each page, lies a voyage guided by the power to create. A force that transcends the restrictions, allowing a writer to follow their daydreams to the fullest. The word "create" itself is a pathway to endless possibilities where words, morals, and so much more, elevate into a gateway of imagination.

This book is a mere testament to the will to create, powered by the boundless potential of imagination. As one is engulfed in these verses that combine into stanzas, that soon craft an overall message, one may find the inspiration to go beyond the limitations and be soon able to embrace the essence of self-expression and creativity.

Still Standing...

Looking at the flag waving,

Glaring at the red I'm smearing,

I am looking all around,

Looking at the flowers falling to the ground,

People weeping ,

Men firing,

The world turned upside down,

Children having a nervous breakdown,

Terror is lurking,

Horror is clouding,

Run before it's too late,

Open and close the gates,

Poof. Lights out.

War is coming no doubt,

Peace for all humanity,

May there be peace and harmony,

Many dangers and obstacles to face,

But it's a slow and steady race.

Lives at cost,

Yet we are still here standing strong.

Endless Daydreams

Glistening lights flowing,
In the euphoric moonlight,
Delicate beings swimming,
In the steady rivers tonight.

Starlight reflecting,
On the pool of diamonds in my eyes,
Eccentric wonders nearby,
Keeping me up till midnight.

My imagination, lingering,
Like a shadow that creeps,
Saying goodbye to the problems,
Above the serene clouds of my mind.

Pondering and pondering,
Until I take a permanent stay,
In my small but fantasy
Of a getaway.

Glued to a never-ending reverie
Making myself never focusing,
About the colorless ideas around me,
No living tension, no unnecessary frustration.

This is what I'd like to call,
My endlessly,
Beautiful, beautiful
Imagination.

Hours of Midnight

The dark ink starts to spread
When you lay your head,
You look out the window,
You watch what follows…

When the celestial being rises from the light,
A new version of life begins,
It starts to become a starry night,
The brightness takes its wings,
Now the serene moon appears with its might.

When all the creatures go to take a rest,
From their awfully busy day,
A cluster of connccting stars starts to express
The different shapes that are displayed,

Without the power of the night sky,
One can never be in the presence of tranquility,
It's the time to be in a calm state of mind,
With the hours of midnight.

Radiate

When the essence of the twilight's shroud is being spread,
Out blooms tiny dots of beaming light under its shed.
Even when half the world is immersed in shadows,
Small specks of light start to follow.

Between the rock-hard cement blocks,
Out emerges a healthy & vibrant floret,
Even in the most gloomiest times, something takes a knock,
Flamboyant hues ameliorate, never taking a rest.

Even at the utter bottom of someone's deepest despairs,
It is promised that a gleaming sensation will be set ablaze,
Creating internal peace, allowing the negativity to tear,
Signifying a ray of hope, deeming to radiate.

A Sister; An Elevation of A Friend

You unbinded me from the nightmares,
Protected my armored fate with a smile,
Told me to soar across the skies without a scare,
Lended me the idea of being versatile.

It was never a moment of "you needed me",
Or "I needed you" in the way I see,
But rather "We needed each other"
And in that, I agree.

As time plays its role in the circle of life,
You're being drifted forward by the waves of
growth,
I'll never forget the angel that gave me wings to
fly,
Our connection will never pause, that I know.

I shall pay you back with all the generosity
You have given all these years to me.
Karma is true and I am ready to give you,
The happiness you gave me once too.

Reality; A Bird's Perspective

My delicate wings allow me to soar across the
skies,
Soft, airy clouds reside by me,
Wind caressing my feathers as I ride in the
sunlight,
Below me would be the tranquility I hope to see.

However…

Chaos invades Mother Nature like an ugly
plague,
Greed and betrayal spread like wildfire,
Oh, how it hurts to see the painful reality win &
separate
From all my positive desires.

Majestic creatures now scarred,
Running, and running from the harshness,
This new humanity has broken Mother Nature's
bond,
I'm fortunate to fly far away from the madness,

I wish for the coming generations to realize,
And effectively cease this harsh abnormality,
That's causing my land to become destroyed,

As this is the harsh bind scarred reality.

Him

He is similar to the lamp that guides me,
In the treacherous seas,
With its vivid and brilliant lights,
And never gives up with all his might.

The sunrise in the light of day,
That gives life and is never astray,
The gold waiting at the end of the rainbow,
Iridescent and unique like a halo.

Always protects and loves,
Keeps his loved ones above all problems,
Willing to sacrifice,
With no strife.

Between him & a superhero,
You cannot differ.
This astonishing figure,

Is a father.

Forward

I used to watch my younger self,
Through memories I found in myself.
Nowadays I ponder about the future
That either holds terror or treasure.

Oh how the times flew by,
Wasn't able to tell with my eyes,
I don't think I have the brawn,
To handle my loved ones moving on.

Time and I, weren't always comrades
But now I have to accept that
I cannot always wish to go back
To the memorable past.

I will always cherish
But not hopelessly wonder.
In the end, I always know
That there is only one way to go,

And that is forward.

Monsoon; A Dewy Experience

The unsettling, foggy climate enters the scene,
An arrival of transparent dews appear from the
sky,
Another one of nature's scheme
For the "harshness" that is soon to dry.

However, the negative side fades away,
As this portrays beauty from the paradise above.
Rain produced from a luxury of white
castaways.
Covering the brightest star of all.

Under the endless wonders from up high,
Are a rainbow of shades in the form of circles.
Individuals protected by raining skies
With an item that could be in the color of purple.

The pervading beauty brings a shine
In it supposed negativity.
There is a truth along these lines.
That's the glorified ecstasy monsoon brings.

Sunflower

A cool shine reflects on me after the night.
I dance to the brisk, sweet air as it coils around
me,
Turning my crown to my source of light.
Nimble birds fly so high, that is what I see.

Imbued with warmth as youthful animals emerge
from their shadows.
From a tiny seed, I sense this season of
beginnings.
Happy that I am a part of a vivid meadow,
Spreading bright smiles as the birds are singing.

Seeing a bee darting towards me, I give it a gift,
Among the meadow with my peers, I see
humans roaming,
Without its nectar, the creature suddenly drifts.
A young human skipped to me with a face,
gleaming,

Touching my petals with grace.
A call came from a great distance,
She then wandered away,
She looked back with resistance.

The bright orange starts to fade,
The sky turns into a dark shade,
With little white specks, wanting to invade,
The light starts to bow with amazing grace,

I soon hope to feel this sensation another day.

We All Matter

An action pierced through many lives,
The shiver in your bones when the danger has
arrived,
Praying to God for a miracle because that is all
you got,
But they were never to be seen again and all was
lost,
Why is the world so dark?

Roads filled with crowds with signs held up
high,
Innocents lost their lives,
We won't back down, this is our fight,
"Black Lives Matter"
Why does equality in this world shatter?

We are standing on the same planet
Let us not make this judgment a habit,
People are separated by the color of their cover,
We all are humans so tell me what's the matter?
He proclaimed, "I have a dream"
Following those simple words, it filled us with
hope,
A person pleaded, "I can't breathe."
We cried endlessly, with a scar in our hearts.

We have to been taught to find a key for every
lock,
Let's stand up and not linger in shock,
So many questions and yet we still cannot
answer,
Let's be proud because we all matter.

Benevolence

I, benevolence will…

Illuminate a soft glow,
Casting a shade of warmth
Upon the world.

Elegant hues radiate,
From the act of giving,
A warm new gradient,
I start this fresh beginning.

I cover the world in a soft blanket,
of mere generosity,
I am the key to every locket,
Fading all monstrosity.

I am the happy ending
To every story,
But not the tale of Earth, for its doom is
impending.

My soft glow fades,
Casting an external darkness,
Upon this domain.

Dull tones exemplify,
From the act of madness,
A harsh gradient electrify,
My beginning, now forgotten.

My soft blanket is ripped apart,
From mere dishonesty,
I was once the key to every locket,
But now it has broken, spreading cruelty.

I wish to be the joyous beginning again,
Could you start by making this wish come true,
my friend?

Serendipity

Gentle brush strokes
Along the dry, rough canvas,
Dull colors like ominous smoke,
Portraying a domain of eerie sadness.

And it continues…

Clashed in a fate of dystopia,
Seems although the idea of faith has been
crushed,
The world runs on all phobias,
Day and night the world wept.

Until…

Amongst was a bright palette,
It soon stumbled,
Toppled,
Tumbled,
Tottered,
All over the canvas, a now a new, improved
planet,

It seems like a dancing force of light
transcended,

Anything in the paint's path had elevated,

In the most childish glee,
Hope was out of its cage, now free.

As if this painting was full of twists and turns,
The renowned harmony now returned,
Healing hope's harsh burns,
As if it's time to embrace the unexpected.

The beauty in this realm of chance,
One must believe in,
As this mere painting reveals a glance
of fortune's magic from within.

A happy coincidence perhaps?
Or even a joyful accident,
Casting a moment of luck in its lapse,
Leaving behind moments of euphoria, and,

Brightens a day whimsically,
Aimlessly,
Joyfully,
This is known as, serendipity.

...happy?

I want to embrace the embers of a phoenix,
Ride the luminescent waves of the sea,
Swirl across the world, in the shape of a helix,
And stumble across a magical forest, carefree.

Oh, but I also want to travel in the domains of time,
Be a graceful artist in the Renaissance era,
Bask in the glory of sunlight as the birds chime,
And be a fierce warrior to slay the Chimera.

But now I need to have a well-paying job,
A successful career, built from a top college,
A 4.0 GPA, and tens of extracurriculars on top,
Working hard, telling me, "It's gonna be worth it".

I need to mask away my imagination,
To focus, and learn things I'll probably never use,
So what's the point of its interpretation?
But I'm still sitting at the front of a classroom,
like a dull muse.

Despite all the reveries that are highly lively,

And the colorless topic of math, which makes
me slightly angry,
I guess throughout it all I'm still a person who
wants to be …happy?

I Am My Own Perfection

She's standing in front of her reflection,

Portrays her face as some sort of rejection,

All it appears to be is a lack of complexion

Errors after errors, leading to a muse of
imperfection,

Drowsy eyes, her skin dries, she thinks that she's
beauty's deflection

But when others look into the mirror, they're the
epitome of perfection,

So what is this? A mirror of manipulation?

Little did she know, across the concrete wall of
construction,

Beyond all the limitations,

Stands a glowing aura of conviction,

It bends the waves of perception,

Into one of lack of tension.

The aura slid into her mind, breaking all
negative restrictions.

She then started to question,

"What am I thinking? What is this guideline of
perfection that I mention?"

In the length of her arms, the stride in her step,
her past negativity is an objection,

In the locks of her hair, the spark in her eye,
confidence now takes an intersection,

In the palm of her hand, the light in her smile,
she now takes a new direction,

This insecurity of manipulation will not dictate,
as I am my own perfection.

Better With You; A Letter to My Mom

More than the stars in the universe,
Is my loyalty to you,
Frustrating days or worse,
I'll still be there, with you.

Generosity and aroma of hope roams the room,
When you're here,
You rescue the house out of gloom,
Here and there.

Strangled with the ropes of stress,
I try everyday to set you free,
Trying to get a smile out of the mess,
You soon become carefree.

Your smile lights the worlds
And beyond,
Your happiest moments,
Are what keeps me fond.

From 7 hours of boredom,
I am ecstatic to see you,
When I come home,
You remind me of a star in a revue.

I hope today,
You're happier than ever,
Without you, the world is like a gray display,
But with you, you make the world so much
better.

Smiled

A fate of dystopia crept along the lines of his
innocence,
An innocent boy, as the light in this world of
darkness,
His hair was like melting gold, a true
blissfulness,
Yet the world he lived in was pure vileness.

As he grew up, his luminescent blue eyes
searched for a new world,
One of peace & harmony, glowing despite
anything stone-cold,
Flowers would dance gracefully, rather than
wilt, and fold,
He would scurry along freely, without a scold.

Soon, he stepped out of these rigid borders,
That stood tall, and ominous all in order.
A small breeze swept by, like serene waters,
Slowly opening his eyes, he felt as if he had
gone in a portal.

Despite all the years of hatred,
His potential for happiness skyrocketed
As what he saw in front of him,

Defied all the dark moral compasses.

This mere act of stepping out of disdain,
Shows there's a lock for every key, a joy you can regain,
All you have to do is breathe, and believe you can reign,
Reign over the restrictions that are inhumane,
Never let your joyous self drain.
Because what this boy did after entering what seemed like a domain,
Was a rare occasion to gain..

Why? Simple,

He smiled without ending in vain.

Rescue

Tick.
Tock.
The eerie clicks of the clock,
The whirling noise of the fan was nonstop,
The creaking chairs sounded like a thousand
knocks,
It has never felt so loud.

Their legs were shaking,
Their hand was trembling
It was all just a sense of anxiety.

Felt like a shadow basking in their worries,
Felt like one in the large, dark sea,
Felt like an eclipsed light, that's what they
believe.

As if being in a room with no windows,
After every twist and turn there's no exit to
follow,
Darkness seeps the room, a heart now with a
hollow.
Everywhere is just indefinite sorrow.

However…

There comes a light at the corner of the room,
A seemingly new profound hope that blooms,
It's a.. Person? No no… it's a foe, a friend to the
rescue.

Everywhere is now just indefinite glee,
Happiness seeps the room, a heart now free,
After every twist and turn there's an exit, a
chance to happily flee.
It's as if they're in the brightest room, the
childish glee, is all they see.

With the comfort of someone new, they feel like
a luminescence,
Felt like one with their loved ones in a meadow
of roses,
Felt like an angel basking in their happiness.

Their hands were out freely,
Their legs were running,
It was all just a sense of being free.

It has never been so soft.
The swaying chairs had rocked,
The fan had all the kids waiting for the fresh air
to start,
The rhythmic clicks of the clock.
Tick.
Tock.